Independent Fluency Practice Passages
Monologues & Dialogues

FLUENCY

Grade 2

Newmark Learning • 629 Fifth Avenue • Pelham, NY • 10803

Fluency Passage Reading Levels

The reading levels of the passages in each Independent Fluency Practice Series book span at least two and as many as five grades.

The purpose of including a wide range of reading levels is to accommodate students in Grades 1, 2, or 3 who read at different levels, and allow them to develop at their own pace. In addition, the wide range allows for students' natural growth and reading improvement during the school year. As students become better readers, they can practice with fluency passages at increasingly higher reading levels.

Book	Reading Levels	Grade-Level Equivalent
Grade 1 **Monologues & Dialogues**	D–E	K, 1—1st half
	F–G	1—1st half
	H–I	1—2nd half
Grade 1 **Fiction & Nonfiction**	J–K	2—1st half
	L–M	2—2nd half
Grade 2 **Monologues & Dialogues**	F–G	1—1st half
	H–I	1—2nd half
	J–K	2—1st half
Grade 2 **Fiction & Nonfiction**	L–M	2—2nd half
	N-O-P	3
Grade 3 **Monologues & Dialogues**	H–I	1—2nd half
	J–K	2—1st half
	L–M	2—2nd half
Grade 3 **Fiction & Nonfiction**	N-O-P	3
	Q–R	4

Table of Contents

Welcome to Newmark Learning's Independent Fluency Practice Passages Series. Each grade-level Monologues and Dialogues title in this series provides 28 carefully leveled practice passages at a range of levels to accommodate on-, below-, and above-level readers. You'll find poems, speeches, editorials, dramas, tongue twisters, letters, and many other text types designed to encourage expressive reading skills. Watch your students learn to vary their phrasing, pacing, intonation, and expression to convey drama, excitement, anticipation, mystery, humor, and more. These passages provide both independent and partner reading opportunities.

Each book comes with an audio CD that provides a fluent reading of each passage so that students can listen and read along to build fluency and comprehension. All reading passages connect to grade-appropriate Science and Social Studies content or fiction genres.

Fluency Research

Fluency is the ability to read a text accurately and quickly. Fluent readers recognize words automatically. They group words into phrases to help them gain the meaning of what they read. Fluent readers also read aloud using prosody—the technical term for reading with expressiveness—with little or no effort.

Fluency is a vital skill because it directly relates to comprehension, and research from the National Reading Panel concludes that repeated oral reading practice at students' independent reading levels is essential to build fluency.

Getting Started:

❏ **Make copies of passages at the student's independent reading level.** You will find the reading level in the upper right corner of each passage.

❏ **Make a copy of the Fluency Self-Assessment Master Chart and Fluency Rubric** (pages 61–62) for each student. If possible, provide a folder in which to store the forms.

❏ **Make a copy of the "Student Instructions" on page 63.** Glue them onto a piece of cardboard.

❏ **Choose a place for the student to work.** Place the copied reading passages, self-assessment charts, graphs, student instructions, a portable CD player, and a stopwatch nearby.

❏ **Demonstrate each step.** Allow students to practice with your help until the process is automatic.

Three Poems About Rain

It's Raining, It's Pouring

It's raining, it's pouring.
The old man is snoring.
He bumped his head,
and he went to bed,
And he couldn't get up
in the morning.

over

Rain, Rain, Go Away
by Mother Goose

Rain, rain, go away.
Come again some other day,
Little Johnny wants to play.

The Rain
by Robert Louis Stevenson

The rain is raining all around.
It falls on field and tree.
It rains on the umbrellas here,
And on the ships at sea.

Self-Check

What do you like to do on a rainy day?

Looking at Clouds

Reader 1: I could sit here all day. I love to look at the clouds.

Reader 2: Me, too. I like to find shapes in the clouds.

Reader 1: Me, too! I see a cloud shaped like a tree.

over →

Reader 2: I see a cloud shaped like a shoe.

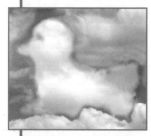

Reader 1: I see a duck. I think I see a boat.

Reader 2: Do you see a hat? Do you see a coat?

Reader 1: A hat or a coat? No. I do not see a hat or a coat.

Reader 2: Too bad. We will need them. It is starting to rain.

Self-Check

Tell about a time you looked for shapes in the clouds. What did you see?

Street Fair Coming to Town

STREET FAIR
May 15
10 A.M.
"Spring Thing"

Green Hill is having a street fair. The fair will be on May 15. Come to Main Street at 10 A.M. Stay until 8 P.M.

The name of the street fair is Spring Thing. You will see flowers everywhere. You will hear music. Tom's Band will play at 2 P.M. Get set to dance!

over

You can eat at the street fair. You can play games. You can even ride a pony! The rides are free for kids.

You can buy things at the street fair. You can sell things, too. You can sell things you have made. If you are a seller, go to town hall first. You must pay ten dollars for a seller's table at the fair.

See you at the street fair!

Self-Check

What part of the street fair would you like most?

City Sights and Sounds

Reader 1: A city has so many things to see.

Reader 2: A city has so many sounds to hear.

Reader 1: "Beep, beep, beep! Out of my way!" say all the car horns.

Reader 2: "Watch where you are going!" say the people in the street.

over →

Reader 1: "Ding-ding-ding!" says a fire truck. The fire truck is going fast.

Reader 2: "I hope everything is okay!" say the people in the street.

Reader 1: "Help, help, help!" calls a little girl. "Save Mr. Fluffy!"

Reader 2: The fireman goes up a tree. The fireman gets the little girl's cat. "Hooray!" says everyone.

Self-Check

Draw a picture of your favorite part of the story.

One Spring Day

Dear Nana,

Today I wanted to play inside. Mom said, "Rain may come soon. Play outside. You will have fun."

I said, "Do I have to?" You know what she said!

I took the dog for a walk. Then we played ball. I threw the ball. The dog got the ball.

over

I threw the ball again. The dog got the ball. We did this over and over. Mom was right. We had a lot of fun!

Mom was right about something else. Rain came! We got very wet. We ran home. We ran through puddles. We ran through mud. That was the most fun!

Now I am home. Now I am inside. Now I wish I could play outside.

Love, J.J.

Self-Check
Why does J.J. want to play outside at the end of the letter?

Snow Day

Reader 1: Oh no! I see snow! I see a lot of snow. How will I get to school?

Reader 2: Put on a hat. Put on a coat.

Reader 1: The snow is deep. My feet will get cold.

Reader 2: Put on socks. Put on boots.

over →

Reader 1: I do not like snow. Snow is too cold.

Reader 2: Wait! Take off your hat. Take off your coat. Take off your boots.

Reader 1: No hat, no coat, no boots? Why?

Reader 2: The man on TV said school is closed. There is too much snow.

Reader 1: No school today? Hooray! Now I *love* snow.

Self-Check

Why did Reader 1 change his mind about the snow?

Falling Snow

See the pretty snowflakes
Falling from the sky;
On the wall and house tops
Soft and thick they lie.

On the window ledges,
On the branches bare;
Now how fast they gather,
Filling all the air.

over

Look into the garden,
Where the grass was green;
Covered by the snowflakes,
Not a blade is seen.

Now the bare black bushes
All look soft and white,
Every twig is covered,
What a pretty sight!

Self-Check

Draw a picture of the poem. Then write a story about what you would do after a snowfall.

Sleet and Hail

Sleet: *(bragging)* I am the worst storm. Watch out, here I come!

Hail: You? Sleet? You are just frozen rain.

Sleet: Well, I sting people when I land on them.

Hail: *I* am the worst storm. Watch out for me!

Sleet: *You?* Hail? You are just small balls of ice.

over

Hail: *(bragging)* I am hard, like stones. And I can be as big as a golf ball— or bigger! Would you want to be in a hail storm?

Sleet: No, I would not want to be in a hail storm. Say, look at that big storm coming. It is raining very hard. The winds are moving very fast.

Hail: That's more than a big storm. That is a hurricane!

Sleet: *(scared)* H-H-Hurricane?

Sleet and **Hail:** Hurricane! Run! Hide!

Self-Check

Draw a picture of a bad storm you have seen or heard about. Then tell a partner about your picture.

Time Box Opened

The past came to life today at the James Street School. Mrs. Yang's third grade class opened a time box. The time box was from 1933. The first year of the James Street School was 1933. A third grade class from 1933 made the time box.

A note on the time box said, "Here are things kids did for fun in 1933. We hope that kids in the future like our toys."

over

Inside the box was a baseball. Inside the box was a doll.

"We play with the same toys today," said one of Mrs. Yang's students.

Inside the time box was a dime. Another note said, "Kids in 1933 love to go to the movies. Kids pay ten cents to see a movie."

Everyone in Mrs. Yang's class laughed. "Kids today still love to go to the movies," said a student. "But today a movie costs a lot more than a dime!"

Self-Check

How are kids in 1933 different than kids today? How are they the same?

When Children Went to Work

Reader 1: In the past, many children did not go to school.

Reader 2: Many children had to go to work.

Reader 1: They worked on farms and they worked in mines.

Reader 2: They worked in factories.

Reader 1: The children worked twelve hours a day. Sometimes they worked seven days a week.

over →

Reader 2: The children did not make much money.

Reader 1: The children had hard work to do. Sometimes the children got hurt.

Reader 2: Then people made laws to help the children. The laws said children could not go to work.

Reader 1: The laws said children must go to school.

Reader 2: Sometimes school is hard.

Reader 1: But going to school is much better than going to work!

Self-Check

Talk to a partner about what it might be like to work all day on a farm, in a mine, or in a factory.

The Birthday Money

Dear Nana,

Thank you for the birthday money. You are so nice to me! I love you very much. I am sad that you missed my party. But I know that taking a trip to my house is hard for you.

I thought a lot about the birthday money. I *was* going to use the money for a new game. But I have a lot of games. I don't need another one.

over ➤

I *was* going to use the money for new shoes. But I just got a cool new pair of shoes. They have lights in the heels.

I thought, "I don't *need* anything. What do I really *want*? How should I use the birthday money?" Do you know what I *really* want? I really want to see you!

I'm going to use the birthday money to visit you!

See you soon,

J.J.

Self-Check

1. **What will J.J. do with the birthday money?**

2. **What would you do if you got money for your birthday?**

The Lemonade Stand

Lena: Lemonade! Get your ice-cold lemonade! Only twenty-five cents a glass!

Curtis: Fresh lemonade! Even better than across the street! Only twenty-five cents a glass!

Lena: Hey, you can't sell lemonade here!

Curtis: Why not? This is a free country.

over ➤

Lena: I was here first.

Curtis: Well, I was here second.

Lena: But if you sell across the street from me, we won't get as many customers. We won't make as much money.

Curtis: I didn't think of that. Why don't we go into business together?

Lena: Good idea! You can come to my side of the street.

Curtis: Why should I? *You* can come to *my* side of the street.

Lena and **Curtis:** *(laughing)* Oh no. Here we go again!

Self-Check

Do you think Lena and Curtis's lemonade stand will make a lot of money?

An Ode to Plant Parts

Roots, stems, and leaves, flowers and seeds

Are plant parts that give us the food we all need.

Some root foods are carrots, potatoes, and beets,

Radishes, turnips, and yams—what a treat!

Some stem foods that we can all munch on merrily

Are bumpy asparagus and crispy celery.

over

Some leaf foods are lettuce and cabbage and spinach.

What's that on your plate still? Kale? Better finish!

Some seed foods are peas, oats, corn, rye, and wheat,

But broccoli's the tastiest flower you'll eat!

Self-Check

Draw a picture of your favorite vegetable and label its parts.

Vegetable Jokes

Question: Why do potatoes make good detectives?

Answer: They keep their *eyes* peeled.

Question: How do you change a pumpkin into another vegetable?

Answer: Throw it high in the air. When it lands, it becomes *squash*.

Question: How do you fix a broken tomato?

Answer: With tomato paste!

over

Question: How did the farmer mend his pants?

Answer: With *cabbage* patches, of course.

Question: Why did the cook call a plumber?

Answer: The kitchen was full of *leeks*!

Question: Why can't the magician tell his secrets in the garden?

Answer: The corn has ears and the potatoes have eyes!

Question and **Answer:** Thank you and good-bye!

Self-Check

Pick one of the jokes. Tell a partner why it is funny. Then perform the joke for the class.

All-Stars Make Finals

The girls' soccer play-offs are in full swing. The All-Stars beat the Bay Street Bears three to two at West Park.

The score went back and forth. First, Pepper Jones of the All-Stars scored. Then May Santos of the Bears scored. The game stayed tied until late in the second half. Then Mimi Wong of the Bears scored on a penalty kick.

over

Coach Smith of the All-Stars called a time-out. She gave the team a pep talk. We don't know what Coach Smith said, but it worked! First, Tara Kelly dodged three Bears and scored. Tie game! The board showed twenty seconds left. The fans rose to their feet as Pepper Jones kicked from midfield. The ball sailed over the goalie's arms and into the net.

The All-Stars will go to the finals next week. The All-Stars will play the winner of tonight's Lady Lions and Red Rockets game.

Self-Check

1. **How do you think Pepper Jones felt when she scored the winning goal?**

2. **Tell a partner about an exciting sports event that you have played in or watched.**

Jump Rope Rhyme Time

Reader 1: I went downtown to see Miss Brown.

Reader 2: She gave me a nickel to buy a pickle.

Reader 1: The pickle was sour, so I bought a flower.

Reader 2: The flower went slack, so I bought a tack.

over ➡

Reader 1: The tack was sharp, so I bought a harp.

Reader 2: The harp broke, so I bought a cloak.

Reader 1: The cloak was tight, so I bought a kite.

Reader 2: The kite flew away, so I bought a tray.

Reader 1: The tray fell down.

Reader 2: Good-bye, Miss Brown!

Self-Check

1. **Create a new last line to rhyme with "The tray fell down."**

2. **Share another jump rope rhyme with a partner.**

Here's to Plants

Attention all humans,
this fact is worth knowing.

Plants give off oxygen
as they are growing.

Each breath we take
helps keep us alive.

If we didn't have oxygen,
we couldn't survive.

over

So say thanks to plants,
with their beautiful greenery.

They do so much more
than improve the scenery.

Self-Check

1. **What is the main reason plants are being celebrated in this poem?**

2. **Talk with your partner about other reasons plants are so important.**

Moth Cheers Up

Butterfly: Hi, cousin Moth. Why are you so sad?

Moth: You have a good life, cousin Butterfly. Your wings have bright colors. People like you. People chase after you. I am not pretty like you.

Butterfly: True, I do have colorful wings. But you are pretty in your own way.

Moth: Me, pretty? How?

Butterfly: You have feathery antennas. I have little bumps on my antennas.

over

Moth: Wow, I do have pretty, feathery antennas. But my life is boring. No one chases after me.

Butterfly: Well, it is not always fun to be chased. I get tired of flying away from butterfly nets.

Moth: You should fly around at night, like me. People can't chase you in the dark.

Butterfly: That sounds like fun. But I don't get to stay up late like you, Moth.

Moth: You should try it! You can go out with me and my friends one night. All the moths hang around at this yellow lightbulb. It's at our favorite place. We call it "The Front Porch."

Self-Check

Would you rather be a butterfly or a moth? Why?

Mount Saint Helens

Dear Diary,

Today is May 18, 1980. I am lucky to be alive to tell you what happened.

I was on an early morning hike in the Cascade Mountains. These mountains are in the northwestern part of the United States. Many of the mountains are volcanoes. Now, can you guess what happened?

over →

At 8:30 this morning, I heard a loud BOOM! One of the mountains blew up! A volcano had erupted. As I said, I was lucky. I was twenty miles away. But I saw the blast. A huge, gray cloud of ash went up, up, up into the sky.

Later that day, I learned that the exploding mountain was Mount Saint Helens. I learned that the ash rose more than twelve miles in the air.

The blast was powerful. The blast knocked down trees. It was so hot that snow on the mountain melted. Now the melted snow is flooding houses, roads, and bridges.

I will remember this day for as long as I live.

Self-Check

Imagine that you are the writer. Draw a picture of what you saw on May 18, 1980.

Rock and Wind

Rock: (*sadly*) Oh, look at me! I used to be a huge, thick rock. Now I am thin in the middle with a big head. And it's your fault!

Wind: Me? Why is it my fault?

Rock: (*angrily*) You are Wind! You blow sand at me. The sand breaks off tiny bits of my rock.

Wind: Then you should be mad at the sand, not at me.

over ➤

Rock: Maybe . . . But after the sand grinds off bits of rock, you blow those bits away. I'm a victim of erosion!

Wind: Wow—I didn't know I was doing that to you, Rock. I'm sorry.

Rock: I guess I shouldn't be mad at you. Erosion happens all over Earth. I owe you an apology.

Wind: Thanks, Rock . . . You know, I like your new look.

Rock: Really?

Wind: Yes, and so do all those people with cameras. They are coming here to take your picture!

Self-Check

Draw a huge, thick rock. Then draw another shape the rock might change to because of erosion.

The Jumblies
A Nonsense Rhyme

by Edward Lear

They went to sea in a Sieve, they did,
In a Sieve they went to sea:
In spite of all their friends could say,
On a winter's morn, on a stormy day,
In a Sieve they went to sea!

over

And when the Sieve turned round and round,
And every one cried, 'You'll all be drowned!'
They called aloud, 'Our Sieve ain't big,
But we don't care a button! we don't care a fig!
In a Sieve we'll go to sea!'

Far and few, far and few,
Are the lands where the Jumblies live;
Their heads are green, and their hands are blue,
And they went to sea in a Sieve.

Self-Check

What do you think will happen in the lands where the Jumblies live?

The Bragging Forests

Warm Forest: I am a warm forest. I am at the bottom of the mountain. I think that I am the best type of forest!

Cold Forest: I am a cold forest. I am higher up the mountain. I think that I am a pretty good forest, too.

Warm Forest: I have maple trees. I have oak trees. I have elm trees. The leaves on my trees are wide.

Cold Forest: I have pine trees. I have fir trees. I have spruce trees. The leaves on my trees are narrow. They are like needles.

over

Warm Forest: In the fall, the leaves on my trees change color. The leaves turn from green to red, yellow, orange, and brown. Beat that, cold forest!

Cold Forest: Hmm . . . The leaves on my trees stay green all year long. That is why my trees are called "evergreens." The leaves on my trees do not change color in the fall.

Warm Forest: That proves that I am the best forest.

Cold Forest: It is true that a warm forest is pretty in the fall. But what happens *after* the leaves on your trees change colors?

Warm Forest: They . . . fall off. Oh, in the winter, a warm forest is *not* the best. It was silly of me to brag.

Self-Check

Draw a picture of a warm forest and a cold forest in spring, summer, fall, and winter.

Breakfast Around the World

The alarm clock rings. It's time to get up. I hope you are hungry. Breakfast is an important meal.

Will you have cereal with milk? Bacon and eggs? Pancakes and syrup? These are popular breakfast foods in the United States and Canada. If you wake up in another country, you might have different foods for breakfast.

In Russia, you might find pickles on your plate.

In Turkey, a quick breakfast is honey-butter spread on bread.

over

In parts of Africa, breakfast is often a thin soup made of ground corn and peanuts.

In Japan, the traditional breakfast is rice served with seaweed.

Are you still hungry?

There are hundreds of countries in the world. There are hundreds of different breakfasts, too. So if you wake up in a new place one morning, be ready to eat new foods. Breakfast is still the most important meal anywhere in the world.

Self-Check

Tell your partner what you like to eat for breakfast. Which of the other foods listed here would you like to try?

Pen Pal E-mails

Sue: Hi, Kim! I just got an e-mail address. I'm sending you my very first e-mail.

Kim: Hi, Sue! Thank you for sending me your first e-mail. I am honored.

Sue: This is so cool. I'm in New York. You're in Korea. But you can write back to me in seconds!

Kim: Yes. As you say in your country—awesome! You're halfway around the world from me. But we can still "talk" as if you lived next door.

over →

Sue: That is so true, "neighbor." It's 9 P.M. in New York. I stayed up later than usual because it's Friday, but I'm about to go to bed. I have a soccer game tomorrow.

Kim: You're going to bed? I just got up a few hours ago! In Korea, it's 10 A.M. *on Saturday.* And I am going to play soccer in a few minutes.

Sue: Weird!

Kim: Yes, weird, but fun. Good night, pen pal. Write again soon!

Self-Check

Write a new e-mail from Kim telling Sue about her soccer game. Then write a new e-mail response from Sue.

The Wind

by Robert Louis Stevenson

I saw you toss the kites on high

And blow the birds about the sky;

And all around I heard you pass,

Like ladies' skirts across the grass.

O wind, a-blowing all day long,

O wind, that sings so long a song!

over

I saw the different things you did,

But always you yourself you hid,

I felt you push, I heard you call,

I could not see yourself at all.

O wind, a-blowing all day long,

O wind, that sings so long a song!

Self-Check

Draw what you see in your mind when you read this poem.

Bad Jokes About Bad Weather

Question: What happens when it rains cats and dogs?

Answer: You have to be careful where you walk. You might step on a *poodle*!

Question: What do you say when it rains chickens and ducks?

Answer: I hate this *fowl* weather!

Question: What did the big hurricane say to the little hurricane?

Answer: I have my *eye* on you!

over

Question: What happened when the tornado lifted the cow into the air?

Answer: It was an *udder* disaster!

Question: How do you find out the weather when you're on vacation?

Answer: Go outside and look at the sky.

Question: What's the weather report for Mexico?

Answer: It'll be *chili* today and hot *tamale*.

Self-Check

With a partner, think of another joke or riddle about the weather. Share it with the class.

Why the Babe Is Still the Best

Many people say Barry Bonds is the best baseball player ever. Barry Bonds has set two famous records. He has hit more home runs than anyone else in baseball history. He also hit the most home runs in one year: seventy-three. Barry Bonds is great. But I say that Babe Ruth was the best baseball player of all time.

Babe Ruth played from 1915 to 1935. He was the greatest hitter of his time. He set many records for home runs that no one broke for many years. What is more important is that Babe Ruth was the *first* player to hit a lot of home runs in a single year. In 1921, the Babe hit fifty-four home runs. That was more than most of the other *teams* hit that year.

over →

Because of Babe Ruth, many players started to try to hit home runs. Since Babe's time, a lot of players have hit a lot of home runs. Fans love to see home runs.

Before Babe became a great home run hitter, he was one of the best pitchers of his time! He set a World Series pitching record that lasted forty years!

The Babe was the best baseball player ever because he could do it all.

Self-Check

1. **Do you agree or disagree with the writer of this story? Explain your answer to a partner.**

2. **Draw a picture of your favorite athlete playing his or her sport.**

TV History

Val: Gramps, did you have TV when you were my age?

Gramps: Yes, we had TV when I was your age. I'm not *that* old! But TV was a new invention then and we had only three channels to watch.

Val: Only three channels? Wow! Today, we have dozens and dozens of channels.

Gramps: The first TV shows were all in black and white, too.

Val: What? No colors? Boring! Why didn't you watch videotapes or DVDs?

over →

Gramps: We didn't have those things back then, in the 1950s! VCRs weren't invented until the 1970s. DVDs are still a new invention. And don't forget that video games, computers, and the Internet are pretty new, too.

Val: No VCRs, DVDs, video games, computers, or Internet? And only three TV channels? What did you do if you didn't want to watch any of the shows on the three channels?

Gramps: Good question! Let's turn off the TV and find out!

Self-Check

1. Do you think that when Gramps was Val's age and TV was a new invention, he would have been bored with only three TV channels? Explain your answer to a partner.

2. If you could not watch TV or use a computer for a week, what would you do?

Fluency Self-Assessment Master Checklist

☺ ☹

Speed/Pacing
Did my speed and pacing match the kind of text I was reading? ☐ ☐
Did my speed and pacing match what the author was saying? ☐ ☐
Did I read with a natural talking voice? ☐ ☐
Did I slow my reading down when appropriate? ☐ ☐
Did I pay attention to punctuation? ☐ ☐

Pausing
Did I pause to keep from running all my words together? ☐ ☐
Did I pause in the correct locations? ☐ ☐
Did I pause for the appropriate length of time? ☐ ☐
Did I pause to help my reading make sense? ☐ ☐
Did I use punctuation to help me figure out when to pause? ☐ ☐

Inflection/Intonation
Did I make my voice rise at a question mark? ☐ ☐
Did I make my voice fall at a period? ☐ ☐
Did I think about what the author was saying so I would
  know when to read louder or softer? ☐ ☐
Did I think about what the author was saying so I would know
  when to stress or emphasize words? ☐ ☐

Phrasing
Did I notice the phrases? ☐ ☐
Did I read all the words in each phrase together? ☐ ☐
Did I think about what the words in the phrase mean when
  they are together? ☐ ☐

Expression
Did I look for clues so I could anticipate the mood of the passage? ☐ ☐
Did I use my tone of voice, facial expressions, and body language
  to express what the author or characters were thinking or feeling? ☐ ☐
Did I change my reading when something new was about to happen? ☐ ☐

Integration
Did I read the words right? (accuracy) ☐ ☐
Did I read the words at the right speed? (rate) ☐ ☐
Did I read with expression? (prosody) ☐ ☐
Did my reading sound like talking? ☐ ☐
Did I understand what I read? ☐ ☐

Student Name: _____ Date: _____

The key elements of reading fluency—accuracy, speed, pacing, pausing, inflection/intonation, expression, phrasing, and the integration of these skills—may be assessed any time a student reads aloud. Discuss the assessment rubric, modeling each description, so students know what you expect.

Fluency Rubric

Rating Scale	Elements of Fluent Reading
	Accuracy
1	Multiple attempts at decoding words are unsuccessful. Word reading accuracy is inadequate/poor, below 90%.
2	Attempts to self-correct errors are usually unsuccessful. Word reading accuracy is marginal, between 90–93%.
3	Attempts to self-correct errors are successful. Word reading accuracy is good, between 94–97%.
4	Most words are read correctly on initial attempt. Minimal self-corrections, all successful. Word reading accuracy is excellent, 98–100%.
	Rate: Speed, Pacing, Pausing
1	Reading is slow and laborious.
2	Reading is either moderately slow or inappropriately fast, and pausing is infrequent or ignored.
3	Reading is an unbalanced combination of slow and fast reading containing inconsistent pausing.
4	Reading is consistently natural, conversational, and appropriately varied (resembling natural oral language).
	Prosody: Inflection/Intonation and Expression
1	Reads in an inexpressive, monotone manner and does not attend to punctuation.
2	Reads with some intonation (pitch/tone/volume/stress) and some attention to punctuation. Reads in a monotone at times.
3	Reads by adjusting intonation (pitch/tone/volume/stress) inappropriately. Consistently attends to punctuation.
4	Reads with intonation that reflects feeling, anticipation, tension, character development, and mood.
	Prosody: Phrasing
1	Reads word by word. Does not attend to author's syntax or sentence structures. Has limited sense of phrase boundaries.
2	Reads slowly and in a choppy manner, usually in two-word phrases. Some attention is given to author's syntax and sentence structures.
3	Reads in phrases of three to four words. Appropriate syntax is used.
4	Reads in longer, more meaningful phrases. Regularly uses phrase boundaries, punctuation, sentence structure, and author's syntax to reflect comprehension and fluent reading.
	Integration
1	Reading is monotone, laborious, inexpressive, and accuracy rate is poor, below 90%.
2	Reading is unbalanced with inconsistent rate and pacing, some phrasing, inadequate intonation and expression, marginal accuracy, between 90–93%.
3	Reading is somewhat adjusted with some variation in rate, appropriate prosody, and with good accuracy, between 94–97%.
4	Reads in an integrated manner with high accuracy, rate, intonation, and expression on a consistent basis. Fluent reading reflects understanding and interpretation of text.

Student Instructions

1. Choose a monologue or dialogue passage for your level.

2. If you are reading a dialogue, get a partner to read with you.

3. Put the audio CD into the CD player. Look at the top right corner of the passage. Find the track number for the passage.

4. Listen to the fluent track on the audio CD. Follow along.

5. Play the fluent track again. Read along quietly with the audio CD. Repeat if you need more practice.

6. Read the passage aloud quietly several times without the audio CD.

7. Answer the Self-Check question at the end of the passage. Make sure you understand what you read.

8. Perform the card in front of an audience.

9. Did you read with fluency? If the answer is NO, practice and perform the same passage again. If the answer is YES, pick a new passage for your level. Use the Fluency Self-Assessment Master Checklist to help you choose skills you would like to improve.

Practice Makes Perfect!